Four-Leaf Clover

Ella Higginson

British Library Cataloguing-in-Publication Data
A catalogue record for this book is available from
the British Library

FOUR = LEAF CLOVER

BY

ELLA HIGGINSON

AUTHOR OF "A FOREST ORCHID," "FROM THE LAND OF THE SNOW-PEARLS,"
"WHEN THE BIRDS GO NORTH AGAIN," ETC.

WHATCOM, WASHINGTON
EDSON & IRISH
1901

FOUR-LEAF CLOVER

TO MRS. H. E. HOLMES

I know a place where the sun is like gold,
 And the cherry blooms burst with snow,
And down underneath is the loveliest nook
 Where the four-leaf clovers grow.

One leaf is for hope, and one is for faith,
 And one is for love, you know,
And God put another in for luck——
 If you search, you will find where they grow.

But you must have hope, and you must have faith,
 You must love and be strong—— and so——
If you work, if you wait, you will find the place
 Where the four-leaf clovers grow.

THE TREMBLING HEART

I lift my head and walk my ways
    Before the world without a tear,
And bravely unto those I meet
    I smile a message of good cheer;
I give my lips to laugh and song,
    And somehow get me thro' each day——
But oh, the tremble in my heart
    Since she has gone away!

Her feet had known the stinging thorns,
    Her eyes the blistering tears,
Bent were her shoulders with the weight
    And sorrow of the years;

The lines were deep upon her brow,
　　Her hair was thin and gray——
And oh, the tremble in my heart
　　Since she has gone away!

I am not sorry——I am glad;
　　I would not have her here again;
God gave her strength life's bitter cup
　　Unto the bitterest dreg to drain;
I will not have less strength than she,
　　I proudly tread my stony way——
But oh, the tremble in my heart
　　Since she has gone away!

THE LITTLE GIRL OF VIOLET-LAND

Oh, tell me where is the little girl
    With the wind-blown hair and the fragile hand,
Who once in the beautiful days ago
    Dwelt with God in Violet-Land?

She talked with Him in her childish speech,
    She walked with Him, and He held her hand;
One might have known by her lifted eyes
    That she dwelt with God in Violet-Land.

But oh, for the word of the baby lips,
    And oh, for the touch of the baby hand!
And oh, for the throb of the raptured heart
    Of the little girl in Violet-Land!

I stand and look thro' the distance far,
My eyes grow dim beneath my hand,
For I seek and call—but I never find
The little girl of Violet-Land.

SEPTEMBER

Purple and gold and crimson,
Lavender, rose and green,
With luminous rays of opal
Trembling in between—
And gold-dust sifted over all
From heaven's curving screen.

THE DARKEST HOUR

The darkest hour is just before the dawn!
 Turn from the deep black valley of Despair,
 And see the roses blooming everywhere——
In the lowliest spot as on the nurtured lawn.

There, shuddering in the wood the sweet-eyed fawn,
 Crouching until the storm has spent its force,
 Then with new courage leaping on its course——
So, when the darkest hour has passed, the dawn!

O Hope——thou shalt not die till Life be gone!
 For he who fights, whatever fate befall,
 Let him be true, and he will conquer all——
The darkest hour is just before the dawn.

SLEEP

O Sleep, come up the hollows of the night —
    My temples throb for thy cool, restful touch;
    My breast yearns for thy coming over-much;
Come up the purple spaces of Delight!

Come like the slow, soft pressure of the sea
    Up tidelands ridged by her own lips at morn;
    Steal, like still winds among the ripening corn,
Across the field Forgetfulness to me.

Breathe like a lotus lulled upon a stream;
    Thrill like a heart-beat from the chastest love,
    Or innocent rapture of a mating dove;
Oh, kiss my eyelids down, and let me dream!

THE CRY OF THE DROWNED

I am dead, dead——
  Down under the sea at rest!
I am drowned, drowned——
  The waves press hard on my breast!
And curious eyes stare long at me,
And all the fishes wonder at me,
And horrible things crawl over me——
  Under the sea, dead.

I am dead, dead——
  And the ships sail over my head!
I am drowned, drowned——
  They sail over my deep, still bed!
And old, sweet faces look down at me,
And old, glad voices float over me,
And loved hands ever beckon to me——
  Under the sea, dead!

I am dead, dead——
*   They cannot see me that look——*
I am drowned, drowned——
*   My life is a closed book!*
And those above see only the waves,
Nor ever think how each one laves
The broken hearts in the lonely graves——
*   Under the sea, dead.*

I am dead, dead ——
*   But oh, this deathless soul!*
Tho' I am drowned, drowned,
*   It sees, thro' the waves that roll,*
The thoughts that no longer turn to me,
And the lips that no longer yearn for me,
And the hearts that no longer burn for me——
*   How bitter to be dead!*

MOTHER'S PICTURE

Laughing, a child, she danced before it;
  "It's mama," she shouted, "why, don't you see?
I thought you would know the very first minute —
  Why, every one says she looks like me!"

Smiling, a maiden, she stood before it;
  "It's mama," she said, and her voice was low;
"The eyes and the brow, and even the dimple,
  Are so like mine; I thought you would know."

Gravely, a matron, she stood before it;
  "It's mother," she said, and her words were slow;
"The lines of care and the eyes of sorrow
  Are like my own — I thought you would know."

An old, old woman, she stood before it,
　　Her step was feeble, her words were low;
"Oh, mother," she said, "thou hast crossed the river,
　　Thro' the lone, dark valley where I must go;
Hold close my hand, for the way is so lonely——
　　Is my soul like thine? And will they know?"

THE MIRROR

I thought I saw Deception in thine eyes a-shine——
Was it but her reflection imaged deep from mine?

SURRENDER IN VICTORY

Lord, we have made an honest fight
    And won the victory;
We fought as men who love the right——
    Fiercely and fearlessly;
And now we turn aside and give
    Our trembling thanks to Thee.

Lord, it is not for us to drink
    The salt cup of defeat,
And victory is glorious,
    And victory is sweet——
Yet still we bow our heads and lay
    Our laurels at Thy feet.

It is not for Americans
  To boast that they have slain
The heroes who have fought and bled
  For their beloved Spain;
Nay——help us to remember, Lord,
  That they have died in vain.

Not sweet can it be, Lord, to Thee,
  But grievous in Thy sight,
For nations to rise up in wrath
  And man with man to fight——
Each thinking his the only truth,
  And his the only right.

But, Lord, the need was——and we fought
  Fiercely and fearlessly;
And still less sweet would it be now——

More grievous — unto Thee
For us to blow the trumpet loud
In boastful jubilee.

So check the tumult of our joy,
And hush the rising cheers;
We have the splendid victory,
And they the blistering tears;
For us the laurel-wreaths; for them
Defeat that burns and sears.

It is the time for thought; the time
For noble silence, Lord;
To-day the mourning-dove of peace
Thro' all our land is heard; ·
To Thee alone Americans
Kiss and give up the sword.

THE STAR

I look across the waste of night;
　　My eyes swim deep in tears——for there,
Plain to my sight, tho' bleak and low,
　　Lies the deep valley of Despair.

Must I, too, walk those bitter miles
　　To that dark mire rimmed round with stones?
Must I leave blood-prints on the way,
　　And lay my bones with those bleaching bones?

I turn and lift my praying eyes
　　To the far sweet deeps of heliotrope,
And lo! a star is coming up——
　　The beautiful God-sent star of Hope.

FOREORDINATION

Oh, but the long smooth waves kept pushing
    That poor dead, beautiful woman to-day——
Kept ever lifting and taunting and pushing,
    Like all hell's demons at play.

Oh, but they lipped at her throat and bosom,
    And slid like a zone around her waist,
And into her corsage, across whose fullness
    A scarlet ribbon was laced.

Two thin dread disks of curling lashes
    Parted the gray snow on her eyes;
Pale were the lips that had known wild kisses——
    Too pale for sobs or sighs.

The smooth, thick ropes of her dusky tresses
    The waves kept winding around her arm,
And around her throat and her poor, bare shoulders,
    As if to keep them warm.

But marvel not — nor murmur "wherefore;"
    Aeons ere she was given breath
The very waves of the sea were chosen
    To taunt her after death.

THE ROSE

She put her arms around Death's neck,
    And leaned upon his breast;
For Life had not been kind to her,
    And it was sweet to rest.

" Poor Heart," Death murmured, bearing her
    Upon her lonely quest;
" Whence came this red, red rose —— whose thorn
    Has pierced thy bleeding breast?"

As up the amethystine deeps
    They mounted to the sun,
She smiled into the eyes of Death:
    " It is my love for one.

" Has it a thorn?   And do I bleed?
      I do not know, nor care."
(She smiled again.)   "I only know
      That red, red rose is there."

THE MESSAGE

Why did I waken suddenly?
      Did a star fall?   Or, hark! . . .
Did a bird call?   Or did Hope
      Set a lamp in the dark
To flame full into my eyes
And signal — " Awake !   Arise !"

MARCH

Hey, alder, hang thy tassels out
   This blue and golden morn;
And willow, show thy silver plush,
   Wild grape, thy scarlet thorn!

And velvet moss about the trees,
   Lift every russet cup——
The dew is coming down this way,
   With pearls to fill them up.

And birds, why tarry so a-South?
   Spent is the bitter rain!
With messages of love and cheer——
   Come North, come North again!

" THEN YOU'LL REMEMBER ME "

You sang . . . The sad years fled like mist,
    The hills were green again,
The lilies opened snow-white cups
    In every wood and glen.

You sang . . . The dark to sunlight turned,
    The skies were blue above,
And every lark across the fields
    Took up the tune of love.

You sang . . . Our hearts were young again,
    Your notes dropped sweet and slow——
And each remembered one whose name
    Must now be spoken low.

THE ROSE OF DAY

The day is opening like a rose——
    Petal on petal backward curled,
Till all its beauty burns and glows,
    And all its fragrance is unfurled.

The day is dying like a rose——
    Soft leaf on leaf dropped down the sky
To gulfs of beauty where repose
    The souls of exquisite things that die.

UNDAUNTED

There is a wind comes at the midnight hour
    Down this bleak canyon deep within the hills,
    So wild, so weird, so strong, it stirs and thrills
My soul, till it is like a shaken flower,
Close-nunneried in some dim old forest-bower,
    That pulls at its earth-roots to leap and go
    Out on the mighty air-tide's ebb and flow——
What time the heavy rain-clouds darkling lower.

Ah, to ride out on such a wind as this,
    Gripped to Death's breast, upon his pallid steed,
    Without an instant's warning or farewell!
To press his lips in one long dauntless kiss,
    And shudder not in any coward creed——
    But face what I deserve, be it heaven or hell!